From Tribulation to Salvation

The Journey of John Fry

By John Fry

Xulon PRESS

I tell you the truth, no one can see the Kingdom of God unless he is born again (John 3:3 NIV).

Contents

Dedication

To My Mother, Allie Fay Fry
July 2, 1935 - August 17, 2009

Mom,

It hasn't even been three months since I told you I didn't want you to die! You looked me in the eye and replied, "Neither do I"! I will never forget the love we shared. I will remember your tender tug on my ear. How we shared in our prayers! Thanks, Mom, for always being there. You often said I was sent from Heaven above with the greatest of love. You always encouraged me in love and prayer. I will always cherish the lifetime of memories we have shared. I know you are safe and secure in the arms of our Lord and Savior, Jesus Christ.

Your loving son,
John

P.S. I promise I will water the plants, change the sheets, and wash the dishes. Yet my number one duty will be to continue serving the Lord. Thanks for your love and prayers.

Introduction

This book is dedicated to you the reader. The story has been made possible only by the blood of the Lamb, our Lord and Savior Jesus Christ, operating in my life. If you are not born again in Christ Jesus, let's get you there before reading further. It is my heartfelt prayer that the Holy Spirit will give you revelation and wisdom as you read this book.

Please pray this prayer out loud: "Father, forgive me of my sins. Come into my heart and be the Lord of my life. Thank you for saving my soul and writing my name in the Lamb's Book of Life. I pray in the name of Jesus, Amen."

In Romans 10:13 it says, "For whosoever shall call upon the name of the Lord shall be saved." And Jeremiah 3:22 (NIV) reminds us the Lord is committed to the backslider: "Return, faithless people; I will cure you of backsliding." What an unconditional love! A person can't earn it and doesn't deserve it; love is from GOD. Always praise and give Him glory for what He has done, is doing, and will do in your life.

Keep in mind that this world is not your home and you are only passing through it. Always do the best you can for Him and be about His business because He is always about yours. As James 4:8 (NKJV) says, "Draw near to God and he will draw near to you!" This is done only by faith, for without a proper knowledge of the Cross it is impossible for the believer to experience a victorious life.

What an incredible deity we have in God the Father, God the Son, and God the Holy Spirit. Whether this is the first time you have prayed for salvation or you are returning to the Cross after backsliding, God has got you covered.

Wherever you are, it is very important for you to get saved before it is too late. There is no return from hell. You never know when you will take your last breath. So be sure where you are going to spend eternity.

In Second Peter: 3:9 it says, "The Lord is not slack concerning His promise as some men count slackness, but is long suffering to us-ward, not willing that any should perish, but that all should come to repentance."

In other words, God suffers long with humankind, attempting to bring us to a place of repentance. God keeps calling after sinners to be saved and desires that no one be lost without him. Once you've committed your life to the Lord, I welcome you to join me on my journey of faith.

Steel Wool Fear

My first encounter with the peace of Jesus happened when I was having nightmares at five years old. I compare the panic and feeling of fear to dense steel wool surrounding me. The terrible feelings sent me to my parents' bed, with me sleeping the rest of the night with them. I would scream, "Get it off me." I was consumed by the steel wool and feared suffocating from it.

I told my mother that I didn't want to die, that there was nothing but darkness when life ended. She said that wasn't so: "There is a savior, His name is Jesus. He won't let anything happen to you." A great peace fell over me at her reassuring words of comfort. I was only five years old but remember the feeling of peace to this day. The nightmares ceased and have never returned.

Memories of Grandma

Throughout the following years my parents forced my siblings and I to attend church. We were not very happy about it. When I was about age nine, my older brother, George, and I, visited our grandparents' home during summer vacation, in Hebron, Nebraska. I'll always remember how my Grandma Fry would pray over us, laying her hands on our heads and giving us her blessings.

Grandma had an enormous Bible that sat on her dining room table and her reading glasses always accompanied the Bible. George and I would pass by her many times during the day and Grandma would be at the table reading and studying the Word of God. Sometimes as we passed by, we would notice her resting her head on the Bible, speaking a language that we couldn't understand. We now know she was praying in tongues.

Innocence Lost

Around age 13, I first started noticing people at church getting baptized in a pool built into the church floor. I questioned my mother, "Why are they doing that?" I thought they were swimming. My mother explained, "They are making a pledge to live for Christ." However, I had no desire to participate in any church activity and was usually in trouble. I guess it was a stage in life that was all about me. But I know God has always been there with me, for me, and watching over me, even though I had not yet been "born again." He has a purpose for all of us.

Through my rebellious teens I began to get a reality check on how real death is. I lost numerous friends and family members. One childhood friend, home on leave from the Marine Corps boot camp and believing he was invincible, died playing "Russian roulette." His father fainted beside his open, shrouded casket.

Losing all my grandparents in my teens was a tremendous blow. A neighbor's father, a co-worker of my father, died of brain cancer. Another neighbor, living on the other side of my parents' home, fell off a communication tower while working, dying at a young age. There were also numerous classmates lost in tragic accidents. It seemed there was one death after another.

When I began tenth grade I was introduced to cigarettes, alcohol, and drugs, and the party started. The workplace of my first real job was overrun with drug use. I was 16 years old when mine began. The following years of drug use included experimental and heavy use. I tried any and every drug out there, including uppers, white cross, black beauties, footballs, downers, quaaludes, LSD, pink/purple microdots, cocaine, valium, mint leaf (PCP), blonde Lebanese hash, black hash, hash oil, stink weed, and gold bud marijuana.

I drew the line at "banging," using drugs intravenously, because I hated needles. I had a horrible experience at the dentist's office as a child. The dentist was giving me a Novocain injection in the roof of my mouth and the needle penetrated my nasal cavity. Novocain was dripping down my face from my nostrils.

At my workplace, I had two co-workers, brothers, whom were into hard-core drugs and alcohol. They used needles and were so addicted and in need of a fix that they held a lighter under a spoon to prepare the drugs while on the job. On one particular Friday, I approached one of the brothers about scoring "bud" for the upcoming weekend. He replied, "No problem, come over to my place after work." When he answered my knock at his door he was smiling with a tourniquet on his left arm, and in his right hand he held a syringe, squeezing out the air bubbles.

I told him I would get my smoke somewhere else (due to my hatred of needles). I had a fun weekend and returned to the office at work to clock in Monday. While I was in the office the phone rang and my foreman answered. He spoke a few words and hung up, giving me a blank stare. With tears in his eyes he told me my co-worker had overdosed and was dead.

I may have been the last person to see him alive and what did we discuss, but drugs! I truly believe the Lord allows unfortunate incidents to happen to us to protect us from our own destructive behaviors and ourselves. I am so thankful I hated needles.

Is God There?

In 1994, I went through a serious illness, the cause of which doctors were unable to diagnose. They performed over $10,000 in tests but still had no answers. The symptoms were severe: vomiting, diarrhea, an overwhelming sense of panic, dizziness, and a feeling as though I would pass out. I lost more than 37 pounds in less than 60 days, unable to keep any food or liquid down. I was vomiting 5-10 times a day.

Fighting dehydration and malnutrition, I had to go to the hospital emergency room several times a week for intravenous fluids and injections. The only relief was the Injections signaling to my body it didn't need to vomit. The vomiting was so severe my esophagus was enflamed and irritated.

That condition was discovered after I was sent for an endoscope examination. Of all the tests and procedures, including ultrasounds, I came to realize my only answer was God. I started calling churches from the telephone book listings. I asked every church the same question: "Is God there?" I knew He was the only answer. God knows me better than I know myself.

After calling several churches and starting to give up (they must have thought I was nuts), I found someone with the right answer. The person told me, "God is surely here, what can He do for you?" She then prayed for me and invited me to a tent revival meeting that night for more prayer. The Lord had me seeking Him like never before, as it was a matter of life and death.

I distinctly recall my final trip to the hospital. My wife was driving, as I was unable. I was crying and felt like I was dying. By this time the hospital trips had become routine. I asked as I received my gown if I could use the restroom before they started installing the IV. While in the restroom, I looked into the mirror and said to God, respectfully but full of emotion, "Heal me now or take me home, either way I win and the devil loses."

That night my life changed forever. While sleeping at home I was physically awakened by the presence of Jesus Christ! At 2:45 A.M., I felt my body sitting upright in bed, from a deep sleep. As my body began to rise, I felt the spirit of death come off my chest, go down my legs, and, as I was in the spirit realm, I watched as the foul spirit left through the walls of my house.

It sounded like an eerie wind; it looked like a dark fog-like cloud, if you could picture it. With the presence of Jesus the evil had no choice but to leave immediately. I then noticed that my wife was also sitting upright, but not awake; her spirit man, being in the presence of Jesus, forced her physical body upright. Jesus spoke to me in my right ear, as we sat straight up, for He was between the two of us.

Jesus spoke these words: "It is me, the One who shed His blood for you, and no harm will come to you!" His voice was vibrant with power and authority. He was very compassionate, and brought great peace. I did not want His presence to leave. I watched my wife's body lay back down in this great peace, as did mine. I was lying there crying and my wife turned to me and asked me what was wrong. I told her, "Nothing is wrong, everything is right. Have you ever had the Holy Ghost shakes? Have you ever been drunk in the Spirit? I was there, and more."

I began telling her everything that had happened. She was overcome with the precious Holy Spirit and began to cry. We held each other closely. If you recall, she was not awakened throughout this experience; it was meant for me alone. For days I was consumed with the presence of Jesus. I remember asking Him, "Why me?" Why did He take the time solely for me? I had looked at myself as not being worthy, a parasite breathing good air that someone else should have. I was always thinking of myself first, taking things for granted. But nothing can separate us from the love of God.

While praising Him, I thanked Him in spirit and truth. I told Jesus, "I love You, You have brought me to a new level with You, You are love." I can't explain to you what I felt. It was a feeling like I've never felt before. I didn't want that peace and presence with Him to leave. While talking to God the Father, I said, "I know Jesus, but You, You're my no-nonsense Daddy. You say what you mean, and mean what you say."

I went on to say, "I want to know You too. What is it about You?" He spoke so softly, answering me by speaking to my spirit, "It was me that was in your bedroom." Instantly, I was soaked in His presence, crying and sobbing like a baby, bless God! I had received such a revelation with Jesus actually coming to my bedroom physically. As if it was not enough that He lived, died, and rose again for me, He came to my side to save me from death, before it was my time.

Since then I have come to realize that God allows events to happen to keep a person. If He had healed me with a creative, miracle healing, I would have returned to a world that was all about me. My healing would prove to be one that would take time. My healing would be gradual. He not only knows our future, He is the potter, we are the clay, and He molds us every day.

I continued to press on, going to church four to five times a week. I would attend Wednesday night service, Friday's prayer service, and two services on Sunday. My body eventually became healed. I had had enough of the Word of God in me, and a hunger for more of Him, to not let go. God surely knows how to keep you in His embrace.

Hebrews 4:13-16 says, "Neither is there any creature that is not manifest in his sight: but all things are naked and opened unto the eyes of Him with whom we have to do. Seeing then that we have a great high priest, that is passed into the heavens, Jesus the Son of God, let us hold fast our profession. For we have not an high priest which cannot be touched with the feeling of our infirmities; but was in all points tempted like as we are, yet without sin. Let us therefore come bodily unto the throne of grace, that we may obtain mercy, and find grace to help in time of need."

Flowing With Him

When you read the testimonies that refer to me, please understand that it is all about Jesus. Jesus is working through me, a willing vessel. I am just flowing with Him, and He is having His way. The Blood of the Lamb has purchased this vessel; it belongs to Him. He is looking for willing vessels to use for His kingdom; it's all about salvation. Souls, souls, and more souls!

If you think God can't use you, remember that Noah got drunk, Abraham was old, Jacob was a liar, Samson had long hair and was a womanizer, David had an affair and was a murderer, Jonah ran from God, Naomi was a widow, Job went bankrupt, Peter denied Christ, Martha worried about everything, Mary Magdalene was a whore, Lazarus was dead, and John the Baptist lost his head.

Now, no more excuses! God is waiting to use you to your full potential. Never hold back from coming to the throne. You will receive grace and mercy, healing and deliverance; it is yours to receive. Whatever God tells you, in whatever circumstance life presents, listen to Him. He is in the restoration business.

Because of the blood of Jesus, all the blessings, everything He has for us, is ours. Claim it and stand strong in it. Remember these points: God wants spiritual fruit, not religious nuts. Growing old is inevitable, growing up is optional. If you are worrying, you didn't pray. If you pray, there is no reason to worry. Blessed are the flexible, for they shall not get bent out of shape.

Book Cart Salvation

God is always having His way at a local jail where I volunteer as a chaplain. What a privilege it is to watch the Lord move among the people. He is all about change. While pushing the book cart around the jail one day and answering request forms from the incarcerated, I met six Hispanic men, only one who could speak English. He requested Spanish language Bibles during our conversation about Jesus.

All six men were sharing one English language Bible so I had one man translate to the others, and using that same Bible, they all got saved. What a privilege it was! We prayed a prayer of salvation and the anointing of the Holy Spirit was strong. I just marveled at how He had His way. God has the perfect plan and perfect time. When it comes to timing in each individual's life, I am always amazed watching Him have His way with others.

Father and Son Saved

One day at church there was an 80-year-old man that came forward to be saved at a salvation call. It was a blessing to minister with Donald back in the prayer room, behind the altar. We became friends, exchanged phone numbers, and kept in touch. I was able to visit with his wife occasionally, on the telephone.

He had been a truck driver for over 40 years. He once told me, "John, you know what kind of lives truck drivers live. I bless God that I am saved but I need prayer for my relationship with my family." We visited back and forth and one day I received a call from his wife informing me he was in the hospital and not doing well. Mind you this couple had been married 50 years.

I went to the hospital to visit him. He was incoherent and unable to respond to anything. He had been heavily medicated and receiving treatment for the cancer. I entered the hospital room and introduced myself to his son at his bedside. I explained who I was and explained my relationship with his father. I asked permission to go over to the bedside to hold his father's hand and to pray with him. I approached him, held his hand, and told him, "Donald, I'm here, it's John."

Donald let out a whine; I knew his spirit man was with him. I looked over at his son, who was crying. I went over to his son, put my hand on his shoulders, and told him of his father's salvation. I explained that Jesus had written his father's name in His Book of

Life. I told him how his father had been set aside, sanctified, and no man on the face of this earth could take that away. I assured him his father was in the hands of Jesus Christ.

I questioned the son, asking if he knew Jesus as his savior and best friend. He replied that he did not. Here is where I marvel at the things the Lord does and how He has His way with His children. I watched Jesus move into this gentleman's heart as I led my friend's son to the Lord. I then told him, "What you need to do is confess your salvation."

We both got up and went to the nurses station to get pen and paper to exchange telephone numbers. As I asked for the pen and paper, he blurted out, "I need to tell you something, I just got saved. Jesus is in my heart and I am born again." There is no greater joy than to watch a person enter the family of Christ. He got saved at his father's bedside and soon after his dad went home to be with Jesus. All of the honor and glory goes to my Father in heaven, my savior Jesus Christ. Whom the Son has set free is free indeed!

Black Ants

While sitting on a friend's garage roof on a hot summer evening, my brother and I were getting stoned with a bong. This was my brother's first experience smoking marijuana. We smoked bowl after bowl, getting quite stoned. My brother moved slowly to the edge of the roof, then he climbed down and went into the house. I followed him into the bathroom, watching him opening his mouth and rubbing his teeth with his fingers. When I asked him what he was doing he replied, "My teeth are floating." I knew then it was time for him to go home.

When we arrived home at our parents' house we walked softly in fear of waking one of them and we didn't turn on the lights. My brother went straight to bed, but not me. I had a case of the "munchies" like you wouldn't believe so I filled the biggest bowl I could find with cereal. While eating I felt my skin tingle. The crawling sensation was on my face, arms, and hands but I continued eating the cereal. Being really stoned, I was satisfying my hunger.

Finally, I thought I should investigate the feeling on my skin, so I turned the light on. To my amazement, I discovered I had been eating a bowl of cereal full of big black ants. They were all over the table, in my hair, between my teeth, and up and down my arms!

Needless to say, that's the last time I ate cereal in the dark! I am so thankful my Father in heaven has carried me through these times of ignorance. I was just plain stupid, being blinded by the things of this world. Praise God, He is full of light and perfect love!

Slain in the Spirit

After my coming to Christ, I invited my brother to a church service. I had been praying he would get the life changing touch from the Lord that I experienced. During the song service my brother was between me and another believer. I grabbed my brother's right hand and my friend grabbed his left hand, praying for Jesus to soak him. Jesus came through, as my brother dropped to the floor between us.

The pastor, watching what had happened, asked us to bring him up to the altar. My brother was very heavy, like dead weight, but we lifted, pushed, and pulled him through the church pews. My brother soon was speaking in tongues, as he not only was slain in the Spirit, but also received his prayer language while on the floor. We continued dragging him to the altar since he was in and out of consciousness, speaking in another tongue. Our prayers were powerfully answered, as my brother was soaked with the presence of the Holy Spirit. Praise the Lord!

Fruit of the Loom

I'll never forget an incident in 1980, shortly after being saved the year before. I was in a small Bible study group, where I witnessed the laying on of hands, speaking forth of healings, and restoration of freedom to lives in all sorts of circumstances.

All I wanted to do was be used mightily by God, for His glory and honor. I wanted to witness His awesome works through my vessel. One evening I remember being in one of the study group meetings, without fully understanding everything. Someone was talking about the Old Testament and how to get closer to God. It was mentioned that what worshipers at that time did was pray in sackcloth and ashes.

That was enough for me, as all I wanted was to get as close to God as I could. What I secretly did was find burlap gunnysack, and I am still not sure where I got the ashes. I think the ashes came from my father-in-law's fireplace, but in any case I went down the basement stairs at my house, wearing only my Fruit of the Loom underwear while carrying the burlap sack and a coffee can of ashes.

My intent was to get as close to God as I could. So I stood on the burlap sack, prayed in tongues quite loudly, and threw ashes all over myself. There were ashes all over me, including my hair and even my ears. Hearing my noise making, my wife had come to see what I was doing.

She was laughing uproariously. She could barely get the words out to ask what I was doing. I figured the truth couldn't hurt so I told her I was getting closer to God. I sure am thankful that God looks at the heart. I know I was a sight to behold. Yes, my Father saw the Fruit of the Loom's too. God has the greatest sense of humor!

Five Hundred Pounds of Dope

During the time of my backsliding I had over 500 pounds of marijuana, drying it out on my garage floor. For whatever reason, my garage caught fire and was blazing pretty well. I heard sirens coming, still off in the distance. A neighbor I had not as yet met came running up to me, asking if he could do anything to help. I asked him if he was "cool," while opening up my garage door. The only thing in sight was 500 pounds of dope on the floor drying. We grabbed the plastic the dope was sitting on, ran across the driveway to my back door, down the stairs, and put it in the basement.

When we got it all in the basement it must have been four feet deep. My heart was pounding out of my chest when the fire department, police, and television crews arrived, heading up my driveway. While the fire was being extinguished, one of the firemen was in the corner of the garage and noticed a bush of marijuana I had overlooked. The fireman turned his back and as soon as he did I grabbed the dope and dropped it in my neighbors' backyard.

Needless to say when all was said and done, with my wife in a frantic state, I bagged up the dope. There were at least 15 30-gallon bags full of marijuana. I loaded the dope into the back of my truck and while a friend drove down a deserted road I stood in the back pitching it out of the truck, bag after bag, until it was all gone. That night I went to "never-never land." There was no way I ever wanted to see dope again! With great relief I went home and was finally able to relax.

The following day a friend stopped over and said somebody had dumped dope all over a ditch she had driven by. We didn't say anything; it was no longer our problem. Since then we have walked with God and used all our energy for Him. Where are you going to put your energy, time, and effort? For God or the devil? There is no "in-between," no gray area. You either serve God or the devil.

I have experienced situation after situation where the Lord has intervened in our lives. He talks and walks with us, and moves in our daily lives. God is truly the Alpha and Omega and has nothing but agape love for us. His love is unconditional, something we can't earn and don't deserve. His love is just there for each of us. Just surrender to Him, give it up to Him, for He is worthy.

Witnessing Things Firsthand

The Lord has allowed me to see into the spirit realm on more than one occasion. Once, when the spirit of death left my body, passing through the walls of my house. Dark like a fog, cold and eerie, with no authority the spirit was rendered powerless because of the presence of Jesus.

There was another occasion when I was allowed to see a few demons. They looked like gremlins or gargoyles, and their eyes were far apart. The creatures' bodies were really little compared to the size of their faces and bulged heads. They had very short bodies, maybe three feet tall, and they looked of a very old age. Their teeth were long and pointed, and they had long, curled fingernails. The fingernails lashed out as they gashed at the flesh of God's children. A co-worker, on more than one occasion, could be seen talking to demons. He wanted to be left alone, uninterrupted, while having various conversations with demons in the workplace.

Alexis

Thoughts of my granddaughter's salvation weighed heavily on my wife Leslie's heart. My granddaughter, Alexis, wanted a relationship with Jesus and was full of questions about Him so my wife purchased a children's Bible for her. Many weekends Leslie had Alexis stay at our home so she could read the Bible to her. My wife explained everything she knew about Jesus, answered all of Alexis' questions, and eventually led her to the Lord.

Later, after my wife had passed away, Alexis was riding with me in the truck when a brother in Christ called on my cell phone. He was in need of prayer and so I immediately began praying for him in the spirit. After I hung up, Alexis watched me praying and inquired, "Grandpa, what is that?"

I explained, "It is my prayer language. It is empowerment in your prayer life. There are three baptisms: one is when you are born again in Christ, one is by water to signify your salvation, and one is in the spirit whereby you receive tongues as a prayer language. It builds your faith, edifies you, and lifts you up. It is the perfect manner of prayer, and we need to be praying all the time."

Before long, Alexis, a nine-year-old little girl, began praying in tongues with me, bless God! Now when Grandpa needs prayer, he gets that little girl on the telephone and tells her, "Alexis, I need you to start praying for Grandpa, and she immediately begins praying. Oh, the faith of a child, and the wonder of her prayers. I just bless God for what He has done, is doing, and what He will do for my family's lives and yours.

As Jude 20-21 states, "But you, beloved, building yourselves up on your most holy faith, praying in the Holy Spirit, keep yourselves in the love of God, looking for the mercy of our Lord Jesus Christ unto eternal life."

Our praying must be exercised in the sphere of the Holy Spirit, motivated and empowered by Him. We are to see to it that we stay within the circle of His love, constantly making the Cross it's object and looking for the rapture of the Church.

Christ and the Mailman's Salvation

A mailman in our town detoured through a church parking lot to deliver the mail and I would see him almost daily. Whenever I saw him we would engage in conservation, usually about the love of God. One day, we had a particular conservation about Jesus Christ and I had the privilege of leading him to the Lord right there in his mail truck, which was *way* cool. Oh, how the angels rejoice when one sinner repents!

Galatians 6:10 reminds us, "As we have therefore opportunity, let us do good unto all men, especially unto them who are of the household of faith." The Holy Spirit will help us to share our faith; otherwise we will fail. There are many who are of faith, but really do not understand the faith, so they walk in defeat. We are to give them the message of the Cross in order that they might walk in perpetual victory.

Salvation Over the Fence

I was driving down the street and envisioned myself pulling over to the side of the street. I pictured my hands going over a fence and a man's hand grabbing my hand, as I led him to the Lord. I wasn't sure where it was or with whom, but I knew it was going to happen. The anointing was very strong throughout my vision and I knew that it was from the Lord.

After my revelation, I was driving and noticed an older gentleman in his front yard. My wife and I were food bank coordinators at a local church and we had seen this gentleman come to the church on other occasions. That is how we recognized him there in the yard. I pulled over, parked, and approached the fence. I called him by name and asked how he was doing.

He said, "Not so well," with tears in his eyes. He told me his friend had died and so I asked him what had happened. He explained that his friend had had pain in his legs and went to the hospital. The doctors couldn't find anything wrong and he was sent home. The pain persisted so he returned to the hospital and a blood clot was discovered. The blood clot caused a heart attack and he died of complications.

I asked him, "Was your friend saved"? He asked me what I meant and I explained salvation to him. I then asked him if he would like to know Jesus as his Savior. I went on to explain that he would have ever-lasting life with Jesus, and his name would be written down in the Lamb's Book of Life. He answered that yes, he would like to be saved. My hands went over

36

the fence and joined hands with his and I led him to the Lord Jesus Christ, who became his personal Savior that day.

The Lord once again showed me that He knows yesterday, today, and the future. He is in control, if you truly surrender to Him. He is with you in every situation, every circumstance, through all events in your life. He just blows my mind. No matter what comes our way, we will win and the devil loses.

All in a Day's Work at Jail

I had a call from a correction officer asking me to come to the first floor of the facility, which was at one time called "Barney land." It was so named after the big purple dinosaur on television we are all familiar with. That was the only program the inmates were allowed to watch, hence the name "Barney land." The inmates were observed viewing the show to see the impact the show would have on their behavior and gauge how they might interact with one another.

As I entered the pod, one inmate, a huge black man twice my size and with an attitude, asked to speak to the chaplain, alone! The correction officer was obviously unsure if I would be safe, alone with the inmate. I assured the correction officer we would be okay and we left the pod. I began praying as this huge man followed me down the hallway to the elevator.

I prayed, "Have your way with this child of Yours. Through me, set him free in Jesus' name, Amen." Once we were in the chaplain's office the inmate backed himself against the wall and began crying like a baby. I went over to him and held him. He rededicated his life to the Lord and he was praying in tongues before our visit ended.

I discovered this man had a heart as big as he was. He just needed someone to talk to and to pray with him. Have you been open to the needs of someone this week? There are people in pain all around us daily. Be an open vessel for God and allow Him to have His way through you for His children to be set free.

Supervisor's Spirituality

I have many dear friends, including co-workers. Once a co-worker/supervisor invited me into his office for prayer. I felt this was a touchy situation considering he held a supervisory position. I had talked to him on several occasions regarding spirituality. We had discussed baptism, the Holy Spirit, and the evidence of speaking in tongues. I knew my friend in Christ Jesus didn't believe in speaking in tongues. I told him I would pray for him to receive the baptism in the Holy Spirit and his heavenly language so that he would become a tongue talker like me.

He said, "I want you to pray for me but don't pray for me to receive that 'tongue thing.'" We entered the office to pray and I told him there is no weapon formed against him that will prosper and that no one can come against him when the Lord Jesus Christ is for him. I then turned to my friend, looking him in the eyes, and asked him if he would be offended if I prayed in tongues. He said he wouldn't mind so I started praying in tongues. After we prayed, he reached up, hugged me, and I left the office.

We parted on Friday and on the following Monday he told me that he needed to see me in his office right away. I followed him to the office and once inside he told me, "At 6:00 A.M. Saturday morning my body sat upright in bed and I started praying in tongues." I explained to him that because of his "stinking thinking," God knew that it would take something extraordinary for him to receive the baptism of the Holy Spirit.

Jesus actually entered my friend's bedroom, where his spirit man recognized Jesus and caused his flesh to sit up, speaking in tongues. Jesus got his attention. He knew my friend really wanted to be a prayer warrior in tongues but had a fear of the unknown tongue. I told him, "What He has shown you is precious. You keep praying in your heavenly language and you will find yourself being an intercessor for Him. You take hold of that and thank and praise Him for what He has done in your life."

The next day, while I was in his office again, he said to me "John, believe it or not it happened again last night. Again, I sat upright in bed praying in tongues." It's great to be used by God. In our minds we are filled with what I call "stinking thinking." We need to stop our stinking thinking and just study the Word of God. We need to listen to the Lord when He speaks to us and be led by the Spirit.

Acts 1:8 declares, "But ye shall receive power, after that the Holy Ghost is come upon you: and ye shall be witnesses unto me both in Jerusalem, and in all Judea, and in Samaria, and unto the uttermost part of the earth."

Miracle working power is inherent in the Holy Spirit and is solely in His domain. This means giving one's all in every capacity for Christ, even to the laying down of one's life. Without the baptism of the Holy Spirit a person cannot really know Jesus as they should.

Moose

My wife and I ministered to inmates, teaching Bible classes, at a nearby prison. We went every Monday for several months. There were three of us, volunteer teachers, teaching in separate classrooms (or pods as they are called). My class had 22 inmates, as did my wife's, and another teacher's. My method of teaching included asking the inmates to fold a piece of paper in half, write their names on it, and place it in front of them. These nametags helped me remember their names. I then introduced myself and spoke of the rainbow of God's promises to us through His Word!

I hadn't noticed but one particular gentleman was standing up. He was a huge white guy who towered over me and he was swinging his arms from side to side. He said, "So what, let God flood the earth, Moose will float." The entire room was laughing. I told him, "Moose, go sit down, you aren't going to float that long." I later learned he was one of three men who had not yet been saved.

So I stopped the lesson, led the three of them to the Lord, and continued teaching. I developed a friendship with many of them and we kept in touch through letters and prayer requests even after the classes had finished. I sometimes had up to 300 brothers in Christ lying on their faces, petitioning God with prayer requests.

During this time there were a lot of baptisms of the Holy Spirit and praying in tongues happening right behind those prison bars. I'm telling you Jesus

Christ is moving behind bars. When I went to the prisons and jails I anointed them with oil and I sanctified and set aside the building itself for His name's sake.

There was another inmate at the prison who got upset while I was praying. Whenever I mentioned Jesus' name or the blood, (because I believe in pleading the blood of Jesus over vessels and placing them in God's protective custody), this person asked me not to mention Jesus' name or the blood. I could see he was cringing and was tormented to no end. I immediately assumed this man was possessed. He actually wasn't possessed, though he was oppressed. He was truly tormented to no end.

I asked him why that was. He replied that some things had gone on in his life that he could not talk about. I totally understood because he was incarcerated and some things, if known, could be dangerous for the inmates. We kept pressing on in prayer when we met every Monday for weeks. He approached me close to the end of the quarter, held on to me, and wailed uncontrollably. He could not stop crying, but I could sense a new inner peace, and the oppression was gone. Peace and freedom were emanating from within him.

He explained to me what happened. From the time he was three years old he had been exposed to the occult. His family members had been involved in the occult. He had become a high priest, doing human sacrifices and drinking the blood from chalices, while summoning demon spirits. The only reason he knew God was real was because he knew that there are opposites for everything. He shared that he had seen much evil manifested before he knew God was real.

The result was that he could not forgive himself. But he sat up one night and denounced everything he had done in his life that was against God. He even forgave himself for sacrificing his first born, a son, on the altar. When he had denounced all he had done, God allowed him to actually hear the angels in heaven singing. He knew then he was going to be okay. God has that unconditional love that you can't earn and don't deserve so you just accept it. Bless God that He is in the restoration business.

Give in the Name of Jesus

I received a telephone call from the prison chaplain. There was an inmate at the jail that the staff thought was possessed. The chaplain asked if I had ever dealt with demon possession. I had seen it before but dealing with it was out of my realm. I knew that the name of Jesus is what the Word says to use against it. When the disciples approached Jesus and asked him why deliverance worked for Him and not for them, He told them it takes prayer and fasting. I also believe what the Word says about the authority in the name of Jesus and the power of His blood.

So the chaplain asked if I could come to the jail the next day to pray and minister to the young man and I said I would. That night I went into prayer, reminding God, "It's about You having Your way and setting Your children free through a willing vessel, period. It doesn't get any more real than this. Show me and minister to me, let me know what needs to be done in order to set this young man free." He spoke to my spirit so softly, "It's all in My name, Jesus, it's all in My name."

A feeling of peace came over me. I knew there is power in His name. From the teachings of the Bible these things are done in His name. I went to the jail and the young man was brought into the room. The door shut as he sat down. His face was full of red marks and scabs, a reaction to the Mace that staff had been forced to use on him. He had freaked them out by jumping on a table and foaming at the mouth. He lashed out at them, speaking things they could not understand, so they finally used Mace to subdue him. He was even foaming at the mouth when they brought him in to meet with me.

As he sat down he began screaming, "Get them out of me, I don't want them in me, get them out of me!" I proceeded to place my hand on his stomach because the spirit man is in one's belly and I commanded those foul spirits to leave his vessel. In the name of Jesus, I told the spirits that they had no power or authority over this man. These spirits had no place or position and I told them they had to leave in the name of Jesus. The young man began spewing, spitting, foaming, yelling, and wailing.

I sensed when the foul spirits left. There was a peace and calmness in that room and within him. His entire demeanor had changed. He looked at me crying with release and relief and peace. He kept repeating, "Thank You, Jesus," over and over while he held me and cried. Together, we sensed the presence and peace of Jesus.

I told the young man, "Now you've got a clean house, and it's time to fill it up." I then led him to the Lord in prayer. Jesus entered in and filled his house. I told him there was one more thing he needed to do. It was time for him to receive the baptism of the Holy Spirit and the evidence of speaking in tongues. He left that room a sanctified and set aside tongue talking brother in Christ. As I said and always will say, "I marvel at what God has done, what He is doing, and what He will continue to do."

And as John 8:36 says, "If the Son therefore shall make you free, ye shall be free indeed." Only Christ can make one free and He does so through and by what He did in dying on the Cross. Our faith is in that, His finished work; it is a freedom that the world cannot give, and in fact doesn't even understand.

Freedom in Jesus

I was once contacted by a pastor from a local church, who asked me to assist with an exorcism. The pastor knew I had dealt with demonic furies in the past. His good friend was also a pastor and a doctor who had a nephew that was possessed; there were demons and evil actively present in his life. We set a time and place to meet at another local church. He had assembled a unique team. There were four of us present and collectively we consisted of one possessed with demons, a Catholic priest, a Baptist doctor, and me, a Pentecostal tongue talker.

Three of us were brothers in Christ gathered to set this young man free from the demons. We laid the young man on the floor, put a pillow under him, and anointed him with oil. The Baptist was on his right, the priest on his left, and I had his shoulders and head. It was apparent the young man was nervous as he told his story of the demon possession within him. He began his downward slide using drugs, alcohol, tarot cards, pentagrams, and other demonic devices. All his actions were an invitation to the demon spirits.

This young man had experienced manifestations of an evil fog and dark spirits that were speaking through him. If that wasn't enough, his uncle actually heard the demon spirits speaking through his nephew. They both knew intervention was needed to set him free. Each demon spirit was identified and we called them out one by one, all the while holding his body to the floor. There was a profound sense of peace emanating from him afterward. After he committed his life to Jesus I followed up with him on a monthly basis and he was still free.

Neighbors in Christ

I was called upon to minister to a church friend's neighbor. The neighbor was a hard-core alcoholic and a retired railroad worker. I went over to the neighbor's house to introduce myself while he was remodeling his home. We had a conversation and established a friendship. When I left I promised to stop by periodically to visit with him. Our friendship became closer as we grew more comfortable with each other.

He eventually shared with me that he had been diagnosed with cancer. The grim news was that he only had about six months to live. I asked him if he knew Jesus as his Savior and he told me he did not. He said he didn't know how God could ever forgive him or want anything to do with him after the life he had lived.

I assured him that the Lord is a God of love who created him and knows him better than he knows himself. I stressed that God wanted a relationship with him and that God had been waiting for him. It was not only my pleasure but also a privilege to lead him to Jesus Christ, his Lord and Savior. The next few months passed and I checked in on him every other week or so. I eventually received the call that he had to be placed in hospice care, where I visited him and his daughter.

I entered his room and laid hands upon him and prayed. I cursed that foul cancer in the name of Jesus and ordered the cancer to wither up and die. I believe in the laying of hands, and healings performed in the name of Jesus. I left him that day and placed him in God's protective custody.

I prayed God would give him peace and comfort. I returned a few days later and the nurse told me he was no longer there. I asked where he was in a hesitant voice, thinking he had died and no one had notified me. They then told me they had sent him home. He was no longer sick enough to need the services of hospice.

I then went over to his house, and there he was. I asked him what had happened and he told me, "I don't know, but I feel great and I have energy!" He lived more than a year after that. He went on walks, worked on his house, and kept on feeling fine. When I visited him he would be watching Christian television and listening to the Word of God.

The Word says that when you are truly saved, you can just see the difference. Oh, the things He does within us. Bless Him for who He is. Though my friend passed away I know I will see him again someday in Heaven with God.

Parking Lot Conversion

I was leaving a parking lot at a local Chinese restaurant when I noticed what looked like a little black man, dressed in really dirty, baggy clothes. He wore a stocking cap pulled down over his eyebrows and approached another person and his family. They had a short conversation, and I noticed that the fellow with his family gave some money to the small man, who then started my way. He spoke softly, asking if I had a couple of dollars to get something to eat. I offered to buy him a dinner but he said that he was barred from the restaurant.

So I said, "I gave you a moment of my time, now give me a moment of yours. Do you know Jesus?" He said, "No, I have had a horrible life and have been gang raped. I am from Washington D.C., and lived in a basement where there was no heat." I told him, "So you know death and destruction. It is real and it is all around us. You are truly lost without Jesus in your life and the bottom line is that if you die without Jesus as your Savior, you will go to hell for all eternity!"

I then asked, "Would you like to know Jesus as your Savior? Would you like to know that your name has been written in the Lamb's Book of Life? Would you like to know that everything in your past has been thrown into the deepest part of the sea and will be remembered no more?" To my amazement, I soon discovered as the person removed their cap for prayer that I had been ministering to a woman! So I grabbed her hand and she gave her heart to the Lord right in that parking lot that day. Oh, how the angels rejoiced!

Divine Appointment

Shortly after we were saved, my wife and I were driving down a street and noticed a gentleman walking down the sidewalk. We drove by watching him as he watched us. His eyes had a piercing quality to them. It seemed we couldn't disconnect our eye contact with him. His eyes held something supernatural and spiritual. So I pulled over to the side of the road and walked up the sidewalk to meet him. I said to him, "Something drew me to you."

It was impressed upon my heart to tell this gentleman, "The Lord Jesus Christ wants me to tell you that He loves you and is there for you. All you have to do is just cry out to him, let Him know what's going on in your life, and talk to Him." I then asked him if I could pray for him and he said yes. I put my hand on his chest and my hand felt as though it was sucked into his chest and through him. He took a deep breath as he fell backwards. He began to weep, wiping his tears away.

I said to him, "Jesus loves you, I just had to tell you that the Lord Jesus Christ loves you." I gave the man every penny I had on me at the time, which was probably about 15 dollars. I felt compelled to do this even though at that time I was working both a full-time job and a part-time job to make ends meet. Each week it seemed I was getting further behind on my bills but I kept persevering.

We really needed that money for our dinner but it was better to give than receive. When God tells you to give, please obey Him. I knew that I was meant to give all that I had to this man, so I did. I was allowed to witness God having his way with this gentleman. Less than a month later I applied for, and was hired, at a new job. The new job provided over $10,000 more per year and it provided 100% health insurance benefits for my family. In one year, my earnings were over $67,000. The new job changed our lives forever. Bless God!

Gang Members

I do a lot of prayer while walking, intercessory prayer. When leaving my house on one of these occasions, I noticed two men, gang members on the sidewalk. One of them had his arm tucked way up the sleeve of his jacket. He got right in my face and told me, "Get out of my homeboy's face and walk, old man." I first thought about reacting in the flesh. I could have taken their two heads and banged them together.

But I realized that I needed to stay in God's realm and handle it in a Christ-like manner. I would not fight against the flesh but would combat the principles of darkness instead by claiming these two men's souls for the Kingdom of God. I responded, "No problem, this old man's walking." I then turned and walked the other way, praying in tongues. I came against the foul spirit that was within them. Then I prayed against the opposition to Christ Jesus. I loosed the restoration of peace, salvation, healing, deliverance, and the prevalence of God in their lives.

About 45 minutes later, as I turned the corner, a whirlwind of anointing encompassed me. I could feel it spinning around me, pulling at my hair and clothing. It was a presence like I had never felt before; it was my heavenly Father protecting me. Then there appeared three gang members and this time they came out on the street in front of me. One had his arm tucked up his sleeve and he was staring at whatever it was that was surrounding me. He actually gazed above me, watching the presence.

I am not sure if it was an angel hovering over me or what, but the guy literally took off running away from me, not slowing a bit. The other two came to me and one told me to walk. I said, "This old man has been walking, talking, and praying to God, and I claim your soul for the Kingdom of God in the name of Jesus." There was a girl there also, and she said, "He's a man of God, don't mess with him."

Immediately, the gang member's foul mouth stopped and calmness came over him. We talked about Jesus. A week later, I received word those two had been arrested for shooting someone. I was safe because I stayed in God's realm of love, praying for their souls. God protected me from them and showed me once again that He is on the scene, ahead of my every need.

God knows our future while we are still in our mother's womb. He knows every hair on our heads. He knows every circumstance we encounter, every second of our lives. All God ever needs are willing vessels to be used for His Kingdom. There is spiritual warfare going on here on earth. Let us be used mightily by Him and for Him while we are here.

As Psalms 27:1-2 says, "The Lord is my light and my salvation; whom shall I fear? The Lord is the strength of my life; of whom shall I be afraid? When the wicked, even mine enemies and my foes, came upon me to eat my flesh, they stumbled and fell.

This portrays Christ in the Garden of Gethsemane on His way to Calvary. As he looked through the darkness, seeing the lanterns and torches held by those who were coming to seize Him, His heart sang of the quiet confidence of an assured faith. Psalm 91:1 (NKJV) reminds us, "He who dwells in the secret place of the Most High, shall abide under the shadow of the Almighty."

Healed

Shortly after I was saved in 1979, I started getting a horrible pain in the ball joint of my jaw. During a two-week period, it became progressively worse, to the point it bruised under my skin. I could barely open my mouth. As I have stated here, I believe in the laying on of hands and healings. I believe it when the Lord says that with His stripes we were, and are, healed.

During this period I stopped by a friend's house. He was the one who led me to Jesus. He laid me down on the floor in the living room floor and laid hands on me, praying a prayer of faith. However, I left the house as messed up as before and was in horrible pain. I told God on my way out of there, "You know that I believe with Jesus' stripes I have been healed Lord, so I'll just wait out the manifestation of it. I believe wholeheartedly and will receive my healing!"

On my way home, I had this urgency, a drawing, pulling me into a church. I didn't know anyone there and had never been there before but I parked and went inside. There was a woman standing to my right in the back of the church and she began speaking in tongues quite loudly. The others there remained quiet and she stopped and sat down.

A man at the podium stood up and said, "The Lord wants me to tell you that there is someone out there with a horrific pain in your jaw. He is healing it right now and it will never bother you again." Of course, it was me and my jaw never bothered me again. Oh, how He intercedes for us. What perfect timing, when it comes to God. There are no coincidences, just His plan for us. He covers every circumstance in our lives; he is always on time, never late.

As First Peter 2:24 says, "Who his own self bare our sins in his own body on the tree, that we, being dead to sins, should live unto righteousness: by whose stripes ye were healed. This refers to the healing of our souls and our bodies physically as well. The atonement included everything man lost in the fall.

Never hold back from coming to the throne. You will receive grace and mercy for your healing and deliverance. Whatever God tells you, in whatever circumstance life presents, listen to His voice. He is in the restoration business. Because of the blood of Jesus, all the blessings, everything He has for us, is ours. Claim it and stand strong in it.

What an Incredible Walk

Have you ever watched someone drink his or her life away? I was introduced to a man that became one of my best friends. Jim was a hard-core drunk. He loved the Lord, but had a serious drinking problem. I would pick him up and take him to church each week. He would help with the cleaning of the church. He helped after Wednesday's men's group, Friday's prayer night, Sunday's service, and Sunday school.

He was trying but just couldn't seem to get a handle on his drinking problem. He would drink more than a fifth of vodka a day. He appointed me not just executor, but administrator of his business affairs. His drinking got so bad he would be found passed out drunk along the curb. The drinking cost him his marriage and his health deteriorated. He developed serious health issues: plastic veins in his legs, quadruple bypass surgery and pacemaker in his heart, blood thinners, and 26 medications a day.

He was over 70 years old when he moved to an apartment and gave me a key to check on him regularly. He witnessed God moving in his life several times. One of his neighbors came by and Jim introduced me to him. During conversation in Jim's living room, I had the opportunity to lead his neighbor to the Lord, with Jim watching as his neighbor got saved.

As I said earlier, Jim had numerous health issues, one of which was hemorrhaging, causing numerous visits to the emergency room. He bled from his mouth and his bottom. His insides were being eaten from the drinking. I was surprised he didn't die of alcohol poisoning. One day I went to his apartment and he wasn't home so I used my key and went in. In my pocket were a bunch of mustard seeds.

I searched his apartment and found all his vodka bottles. If you have ever known an alcoholic, the hiding places are many. There were bottles in his shirts and coats hanging in the closet, with the cleaning supplies under the sink, in the bath towels, his pants drawer, with the canned goods, and all over the apartment.

I prayed over the mustard seeds in my pocket and put a few seeds in each vodka bottle. I then prayed to God for Jim's deliverance from alcohol. My hope was that Jim would see alcohol as a tool from the devil to destroy his life and would turn away from the alcohol that was killing him. Those seeds were anointed and I put them in every bottle before leaving and locking the door behind me.

A few days later I received a call from the emergency room nurse saying that Jim was there and I needed to visit him. When I arrived there were all kinds of tubes going in and coming out of him. There was blood coming from his nose, mouth, and bottom, and he was scared. When I asked him what had happened he told me he had been out all day, drinking downtown. When he returned home to his apartment he started on his stash of vodka.

However, he told me, "This time it was different." He said, "I'm so tired of this, I hate this, it's ruined my life." He asked me to pray with him and I immediately praised God. I told Jim, "I believe you have been delivered and are free from alcohol. I put mustard seeds in all the bottles I found and asked God to deliver you and set you free. I believe that is what happened to you."

Jim said, "I'm done with it, I am not drinking anymore, I don't like living this way." From that point forward, he lived as a non-drinker. I never saw him drink again. Jim expressed his fear of dying so he rededicated himself to the Lord and this time it stuck. Jim went on to have many health problems, including getting a leg amputated, but he persevered. He woke up at 4:00 A.M. everyday to pray.

We kept in touch and would have dinner together from time to time. He was a very dear friend. The nursing home where he lived notified me that he had gone home to be with the Lord a year after his deliverance from alcohol. I bless God for his fellowship, and the part of his life he shared with me. I know without a shadow of a doubt he went to be with the Lord.

It says in Acts 19:11-12, "And God wrought special miracles by the hands of Paul: so that from his body were brought unto the sick handkerchiefs or aprons, and the diseased departed from them, and the evil spirits went out of them." It was not just pieces of cloth that did this, but rather the power of God operating through the cloths as a point of contact regarding faith.

A Precious Time of Salvation

There are no coincidences with God. For example, I was at the hospital visiting a friend who had surgery. She, her husband, and I had a conversation about the Lord and being right with God. I told her husband that this is not our home and that we are just passing through. I asked if he was saved and he told me no. His wife spoke up and said it was always her wish that he would be saved. She spoke with tears forming in her eyes, as it was something he had never done or felt comfortable with.

I then told this man that there was no better time than the present. The Lord moved upon his heart and I was able to lead him to Jesus, right there in the hospital, at his wife's bedside. What a precious time! I am always in awe of Him having His way in His children's lives. I watched as the two of them embraced, she cried, and her husband became a new creature in Jesus.

I asked him to look into his wife's eyes and tell her what just happened to him. He told her, "I just got saved. My name has been written in the Lamb's Book of Life." What an awesome experience. I had gone from ministering to people in the jail to people on the street to people in the church. I always marvel at Him, who He is, what He has done, and what He is going to do.

Romans 10:9 says, "That if you confess with your mouth the Lord Jesus and believe in your heart that God has raised him from the dead, you will be saved." And First John 1:9 says, "If we confess sins, He is faithful and just to forgive us our sins and to cleanse us from all unrighteousness."

Fishing With the Fisherman

My wife, Les, and I loved to fish. We went fishing all the time. We would take out our little boat on the water to spend the day fishing. One time we were on the river and it was a hot, stagnant day, without the slightest breeze. The sky was crystal clear and it was super hot. The thing about my wife was that her whole life was about Jesus. Even when she would see a wild animal she thanked Jesus.

I'll never forget being on that river and her turning to me and saying, "John, wouldn't it be cool if Jesus sent a breeze down this river just to cool us down?" She then said, "Jesus, I ask You to just do that for John and me this day. I thank You and praise you for it."

We could hear and see off in the distance that the trees were whistling as the wind came down. The tree leaves on both sides of the river were whistling and this breeze just blew over us cooling us down and then disappearing. Les dropped her pole, her hands went in the air, and she started praising Him and thanking Him. I will never, ever, forget it. Bless you Lord!

Bye Bye, Dope

I have had guns stuck in my face and I pointed a few at others also. It really is a miracle I am alive at all. If you have ever done drugs you know what I am talking about. Drugs can cause you to do stupid things. No, the drugs do not make you do anything you do or do not want to do. Whether you are saved or not, it is by your will and that is something God will never interfere with.

In all the years I used drugs and acted with stupidity I truly believed that God protected me. And the stupidity finally wore off! I will never forget being sick and tired of being sick and tired. There finally came a time when I didn't want to use drugs anymore, but I struggled with the addiction.

While I was stoned out of my mind, I prayed to God to deliver me from the muck and mire. I asked Him to set my household free. I was tired of being upside down and inside out. I prayed in the name of Jesus and He delivered me while I slept.

I awoke with a mindset of clarity and freedom. Afterward, I went through the entire house, breaking all the pipes and flushing the dope. My house was cleansed. When He delivers you, you are truly delivered. As the Word reminds us, "When the Son sets you free, you are free indeed."

And as Jesus says in John 10:10, "The thief cometh not, but for to steal, and to kill, and to destroy: I am come that they might have life, and that they might have it more abundantly." The devil will try to use any avenue he can to take you out but God is greater than the devil.

Can't Hide Anything From God

Have you ever lost something and had a burden to find it? It can drive you nuts while you keep searching everywhere. You try to replay in your mind losing the item, without finding it. I had that happen with an antique posthole digger that didn't belong to me. I had borrowed it from a family member and they needed it back. I prayed earnestly, "God, you must show me where this thing is." I had such a burden to find it because it didn't belong to me. I prayed and prayed and finally came to the point where I had a release in my spirit and I let it go. That is when I got my breakthrough.

While I was sleeping the Lord woke me up and I sat upon the side of the bed. I couldn't see it but He showed me who had borrowed that posthole digger. I had a quickening of my spirit and just marveled at the goodness of God. I called the individual and he said he had it. He later left his garage unlocked for me and I picked it up from him to return to my relative. Our minds can only take us so far. If we just got rid of our "stinking thinking" our lives would be a lot better off. God once again showed me that He is always talking to us if we take the time to listen. He always wants to help us.

Angels on the Scene

One of my best friends still remembers a particular incident like it happened just yesterday. He was in jail and had just learned the charges against him were going to total a sentence of 40 years. As he was upset and didn't want to hear the sentence rendered, he became uncontrollable. For making the guards' job much harder, he got put in solitary confinement.

On June 17, 1994, as he was sleeping on his hard cot, at around 3:00 A.M., he was startled. He stared at an elderly man in his cell. The man had gray hair with gray facial hair, a goatee. The man's clothing was a brand of work clothes and he appeared to be the type of fellow you might see just about anywhere. My friend sat up suddenly when he noticed the man in his cell. The elderly man moved toward him, stretching out his hands and signaling my friend to be calm. The man said to him, "You are not here for the crimes you've committed, you have been running from God. If you would just read the Bible and learn to pray, He will take care of your case!"

The elderly gentleman then turned and walked through the 10-inch-thick steel door and disappeared. Just as suddenly as he appeared, he was gone. Then my friend fell to his knees, crying and raising his hands in surrender to God. He said, "I don't know You or what You want, all I know is how not to live right, but I will do whatever You want." He obeyed God and the miracle of miracles is that his 40-year sentence actually turned out to be only three years in a federal prison. He did not have to fight his own case, as God fought it for him. He was completely healed of the drug use and criminal lifestyle he had led. He had to be locked up, to be set free!

Darkness Before Dawn

One day while driving down the highway I noticed items being thrown out of a vehicle. The car pulled over to the shoulder and then a man was thrown out of the car. I passed the vehicle but turned around and went back to it. The man was collecting his belongings as I pulled up to check the situation out. There was a white powder all over the highway so I wondered what I was getting myself into, as I figured it was cocaine.

I asked the man what was happening so he told me he was homeless and had just been kicked out of the house where he had been living. I asked him if I could help and he asked for a ride to the nearby town. I then asked him what the white powder was. The man told me it was his laundry detergent, and I realized then that I had prejudged him, thinking it was drugs. I checked the powder to be sure it really was detergent, and it was. We loaded up his things, got into my car, and headed for the town.

The man smelled as though he had not bathed in a very long time. He was in the backseat of my car and asked me to pull over at the nearest wooded area we came to. He admitted he wanted to find a place to commit suicide. He told me he just needed to die. I placed myself in God's protective custody and prayed for the blood of Jesus to watch over my vessel.

I prayed for salvation for this man's soul and deliverance of his vessel. I started talking to the stranger about the Lord and told him to give it to

God. I also explained his need to be saved. We talked further and he repeated the sinner's prayer. He finally fell asleep on the rear floorboard of my car.

When we reached the small town, I noticed a police officer. I pulled over, explained the situation to the officer, and asked directions to the nearest hospital. I followed the officer to the hospital and when we entered it we hailed a nurse to explain the situation. The nurse came out and woke up my passenger, put him in a wheelchair, and took him inside. While waiting for him to be seen we were told he had not taken his medication for more than a week and he was schizophrenic.

The hospital staff assured me he would get the help he needed so I left him there. He would later be transported to the local hospital in the town where he lived. God answers when we pray and so we need to be in prayer all of the time.

Candy Bar Testimony

One night I went on a walk, in prayer, just hanging out with the Lord. Along the way I stopped at the neighborhood convenience shop. I bought a candy bar and a soda, and continued my walk, munching on the candy bar. When I finished the candy bar, I threw the wrapper on the ground, sipped my soda, and continued my walk in the dark. I remember the Lord spoke to me and asked, "Did I not create all things?" I agreed and He then reminded me that I had thrown that wrapper on the ground. He softly spoke to my spirit to turn around and go back after the wrapper.

I turned around, wondering how I was going to find it in that dark night. I had no clue where I had thrown it, but I started back up the sidewalk, in prayer. I backtracked quite a ways up the hill, maybe a quarter of a mile. At one point God told me to stop, look to my left, and it was right there next to my left foot. I call this testimony my "candy bar testimony." I use this testimony to show how important it is to hear from the Lord.

Jesus Met My Needs

Have you ever had something happen to you and think you "got it" at the time it happened? Later you look back on it and think, *Wow, that's what that was all about!* You finally get a revelation about the occurrence. For example, a few years after the incident in my bedroom, when God spoke to me and I sat upright in bed, my wife was in the hospital, dying. My emotions were very high and I was totally leaning on God as never before. I had recruited people for prayer for her. There were thousands of people praying for Les, through prayer chains, family and friends, all praying for a manifestation of healing.

Watching the body changes as, your loved one is dying before your eyes, is the most helpless feeling you can imagine; you are unable to eat, get severe headaches, are nauseated, and are totally stressed. Mentally, physically, and spiritually, you are hoping and praying for the best. I went on like this nearly three weeks, praying and greeting visitors, and supporting the family. My prayers were for a miracle healing to take place.

My wife and I had our twenty-third wedding anniversary approaching. I asked God to please let her sit up in bed, to be healed. I had plans of renewing our vows. I had thoughts of how great our future was going to be together. I believed whole-heartedly for a miracle manifestation, knowing what God had shown in the past. I laid hands on her and prayed for her to live, not wanting her to die.

I spoke to her spirit, knowing without a shadow of a doubt she heard me. When I prayed I said, "Les, pray this prayer with me. I know you cannot respond physically, but pray with me, spirit to spirit: 'I shall live and not die, and declare the works of the Lord.'" I prayed this three times while I looked at her body lying there, on life support, tubes going in and out of her. I released my hand from hers and she let out a whine. I knew contact was there, spirit to spirit. Our spirit man is always young and vibrant, healthy and energetic.

One day before our twenty-third wedding anniversary, the Lord spoke to my spirit ever so gently that He was going to escort Leslie home with Him, and a great peace fell over me. Even though I didn't want to accept it, and didn't want to let her go, I knew I had to. Les had always told me God had placed us together and I told her I knew that too. We were soul mates and had the deepest of love for one another. We knew that we knew we were placed together by Him. Les told me once that her love for me was so intense that it actually hurt. She knew she could not live without me and so maybe that's why she went home first.

On the day of our anniversary, I was at home in bed. I had just spent another long emotional day at the hospital. Suddenly, I was placed directly on my feet from a deep sleep. I found myself bent over with my hands in the air, screaming out "Leslie." What was happening at that very moment was that her spirit was departing from her flesh. It was her spirit leaving for Heaven. We were such close soul mates that I felt the separation. I had a profound feeling of emptiness, a tearing apart from within me. I immediately began praying in tongues and the Lord Jesus Christ was there with me.

I was totally exhausted from the experience, as her illness had lasted for weeks. As I lay back down, it seemed like it had only been for a moment. Then my vessel, back in a deep sleep, was again upright and I was back on my feet again. My hands were in the air and I was bent over, praying in tongues before Him. At that moment, on our twenty-third anniversary, God brought Leslie to my bedside before He escorted her to Heaven. Her heart's desire before leaving was to see me one more time before heading home. The love of Christ fulfills our hearts' desire. I have no other explanation than what I have just stated. I pray He gives you revelation, from the depth of Him, as he has to me. How great is His love!

God Has My Back

Shortly after losing my wife I often walked around feeling numb. I asked God why I was even left here, as I was devastated at the loss of her, and asked God to just kill me. I felt I no longer had purpose and that I didn't need to be here anymore. God knew how desperate the situation was and that I needed brothers and sisters in Christ to be put in my path. So He sent me help while I was in a remote part of the building where I work evenings.

A teacher approached me and asked me, "John, how are you doing?" I answered that I was not doing well at all. I was sobbing and he asked if he could pray for me. As he began, I stopped him to explain, "I believe in the laying on of hands and healings, and have had many experiences with the Lord. I need the power of prayer." He told me that he was an associate pastor in a local church and believed as I do in the laying on of hands so he laid his hands on me.

He started praying in tongues and the peace of God washed over me like never before. I thank God for placing brothers and sisters in Christ across my path. The timing was perfect, for the staff member would not normally have been in our building at that time. God is always on the scene. He always proves that He is good and He never sleeps or slumbers. How could anyone not want a relationship with Him?

Mom's Prayers

My mother told me on several occasions that she has witnessed Jesus standing at my back door, sometimes with angels standing on each side of Him. Other times the angels and Jesus completely surrounded the house. She also told me she had seen Him standing at the foot of my bed, looking down on me smiling. I have not yet been so blessed to actually see Him, but I have heard Him speak to me audibly.

I pray for the day to come when I will see Him in person. Meanwhile, I have sensed when His presence is near me. Once a person has experienced His presence there is just nothing like it. You want to be absorbed in His presence all the time. Anything other than that is just not sufficient. God placed this holy hunger in me and I bless Him for who He is and what He has done.

Restoration

I have witnessed God having His way with His children in so many ways. While ministering at the jail, I ministered to several of His children at a time. I laid hands upon one man and he began singing in the spirit. He was wailing from the inside out and had a powerful release and cleansing of his soul. I have also led many youths to the Lord and ministered to them throughout their time in jail. I also followed up with them on the outside after their release from jail. I marvel at how God has changed their lives.

Let's go back to an earlier part of this book, where Jesus came into my bedroom. He did not allow me to see him but spoke audibly to me, "It is Me, the One who shed the blood for you, and no harm will come to you." During that entire week I was overcome with His presence. I marveled at what had happened. The Son of God, Jesus Christ, actually took the time to visit me in my bedroom. He came to take care of me and my mess. I wept and told Jesus that I was just amazed at the depth of His love. And it still awes me to this day.

I looked at myself as useless garbage and a parasite, using drugs and wasting precious time. I had been of no use to anybody. I told Jesus, "As if it was not enough that You loved me, You even died for me. After all that You have done, You came to my bedroom to stop what it was that was going to destroy me." I told Him that I had taken everything He had done for me for granted earlier and I was ashamed and embarrassed. Others may have turned me away but He didn't. He came to me in spite of myself. That spirit of death left me when He entered my life. The depth of His love is unbelievable and it leaves me astonished.

Time and Eternity

The time we spend here on earth is nothing compared to that of eternity after we leave here. I see a rainbow and am in awe for I am reminded of His promises. I look up at the stars at night, gaze at the moon, look at the sun, think of the size of the earth, and marvel. Look at the world, populated by billions of people, yet there are no two fingerprints alike.

I pray for my one-on-one encounter with Him. I am excited about meeting again with family that has gone on before me. No more pain, anguish, or suffering, just total peace. We have everything to look forward to there together with our Lord.

I encourage you to get saved if you are not. Get your name in the Lamb's Book of Life. It is the most important decision of your life. Get born again in Christ Jesus. Stand strong in your salvation. There is no one on the face of this earth that can take your salvation from you. This doesn't mean you are always going to walk perfect. It doesn't mean you won't have trials and tribulations.

What is important is not how many times you fall, but how many times you get back up. Press forward and continue to go toward the mark that is Jesus Christ. He is our power, our fortress, our refuge, and strength. It is because of Him that we have all these blessings. We are never going to stop learning of His goodness while we're here on earth.

A Seed Bears Fruit

One day I was ministering to a brother in Christ who had been incarcerated. He requested a Bible and was in need of prayer so I gave him one and asked him what it was that troubled him. He told me that he was seeking a sentence reduction, as he had been incarcerated for 17 years.

I asked him about his testimony and he told me that while he was in jail before being sent to prison he went through the phone book calling churches. He asked them if they would bring him a Bible and come to pray with him. The fellow said he went through several church listings and was ready to give up after being rejected by all of them. The last call the man made was answered by a woman, who agreed to visit him.

When she got to the jail she asked the inmate, "I keep seeing a stick with residue on it, do you know what that means?" He responded, "That is why I am here. I have been charged with manufacturing dope and they have my stir stick with residue still on it." He then realized without a shadow of doubt that God was with him in jail and the visitor led him to the Lord. After he related this story to me, I prayed for God's perfect will to be done in his life and led him to receive the empowerment of prayer in tongues.

The Name of Jesus

In the spirit realm, I have witnessed many things audibly, without seeing the manifestation of the being. While lying on my bed awake and watching television, I sensed within my spirit something foul was in the room. I not only felt its physical footsteps crossing my bed but I also watched each impression of each step being taken, as it walked across the bed.

It was moving very slow, as if it were approaching with caution. It approached me on the left side of my body, beginning at my feet and going up to my head. I had no fear as I lay there. I just laughed and said the most powerful name in the entire universe, Jesus, and it immediately left. Praise Him there is power in His name.

Holy Ghost Healthcare

While in the waiting room for an orthopedic appointment I was in prayer to be used mightily by Him and for His glory in any manner He saw fit. My name was called for me to go to the exam room and the doctor entered to discuss my health issue. I asked him how he was doing and if he had been in prayer, and he answered, "John, I am always in prayer." I then asked if he had ever been around any tongue talkers and he told me his uncle prayed in the spirit all the time.

He admitted he didn't know much about that gift and had never spoke in tongues. I then asked him if he had ever desired the ability to speak in tongues and he replied YES! I explained that the desire he had was God-given. Jesus had promised that He would baptize him and give him utterance in tongues. So with instruction and prayer, on that day and in that examination room, my doctor friend left praying in tongues. His life has been forever changed because of the power of prayer in the spirit.

Childhood to Salvation

I once met a married couple that I learned was saved, and after a brief visit together the husband was blessed to receive tongues immediately. I then concentrated on helping his wife to receive it and while instructing her, I sensed she had placed a wall up to resist it. I explained that one reason a person would not receive tongues is if that person might be holding back.

I also explained that it was Jesus who promised to baptize her to receive tongues. I then asked if she was afraid of something or if there were some other reason causing her hesitation. She told me she was afraid her husband would not be able to receive tongues and the fear must have caused a wall to be placed between her and receiving the Holy spirit.

God asked me to ask her maiden name. I shook my head and mentally asked God what her maiden name had to do with anything. He said again to ask her what her maiden name was. I did as He asked and as I looked into her eyes they stared back at me with confusion. When she finally answered, I was totally shocked.

Once I heard her maiden name I instantly recalled that I went to high school with her. As a matter of fact, we had grown up together. She and I hugged with joy as we realized our connection. Her husband was shocked also to learn she and I had grown up together. The whole atmosphere and mood changed. I instructed her to go home and find a relaxing spot after dinner. I recommended that she go home and take a shower, spend time alone or doing whatever relaxes her and start speaking in tongues.

The following day was Sunday and she and her husband approached me at church, very excited. They explained that when they got home the day before and she got relaxed that she began speaking in tongues. He said, "She would not shut up all night." Isn't God good, all the time? Praise God Almighty!

Return to the Light

A very dear friend and brother in Christ was shot in the head. He was shot because of drugs and the downward spiral of other things that go with the use of drugs. He related to me that he had died and gone through a tunnel. There the bright light was drawing him through to the other side. He happened upon Jesus sitting with His hands in His lap. The brilliance of the light was so intense with glory that he couldn't look into the light so instead he looked at His feet.

Jesus spoke to him, telling him it was not yet his time and that he must go back. He didn't want to leave but awoke up in the hospital, emerging from the coma he had been in earlier. He required extensive physical rehabilitation lasting many months. He is now saved and is serving Jesus at the jail as a chaplain volunteer. Does God have a hold on you? Of course He does! He created you and knew you before you were in the womb. The real question is do you have a hold on Him? Have you surrendered to Him whole-heartily?

How God Changes Bad to Good

My son had an acquaintance that was involved in drugs, alcohol, and various other crimes, too many to mention. He had been in jail and before a judge more times than I could count for everything from drugs to assault, and a rape he was never charged with. He had been warned time and time again to stay away from my house but I pulled in my driveway to find him sitting in his car at my back door. I got out of my vehicle, went to his car window, and told him to leave and not to come back or I would bury him in a field where no one would find him. Needless to say he didn't return to my house again.

I have a nephew who had received Christ and I invited him to services at the church that I attend. He in turn asked a couple to join him. When my nephew invited them initially, the friend (who was the acquaintance of my son) asked in a frightened voice if it was the church I attended. My nephew said it was and then his friend went on to say that he couldn't attend because I was there.

Again my nephew reassured him and told him it would be okay so he and his wife accompanied my nephew to the church. The kid kept his distance, hanging back in the sanctuary and waiting to see my reaction. My nephew told me his friend was there and so I turned and walked over to the young man. I took his hand and we had a long talk. He had straightened out his life and was no longer on dope. I took both he and his wife to the prayer room behind the altar and led them both to the Lord. They know they can call on me for prayer anytime and I check in on them periodically.

"I Cuss A Lot"

One Sunday afternoon at church, a biracial couple approached the altar for a salvation call. He is white, she is black, and the Holy Spirit was all over them. I introduced myself and asked if it was salvation or a recommitment they were seeking. They both had recommitted their lives so I asked if prayer was needed. He said yes, and began crying, adding that he had a heart condition and could die at any time. She spoke up and said, "We both need your prayer for our relationship with each other and with God."

I told her, "No problem, nothing is too big for God." I asked them if they spoke in tongues and she said she did but he looked puzzled. He told me, "No, I don't pray in tongues but I sure do cuss a lot." I thought I would burst with laughter as I struggled to keep my composure. I explained that tongues is the perfect manner of prayer and that God can't answer if we are not praying. We can't do it without Him, and He will not do it without us. What a great love our heavenly Father has for us. We all gathered in prayer and my brother emerged from that prayer room as a tongue talker. Praise the Lord!

Precious Spirit

I received a phone call asking if I would come to the Veterans Hospital in Knoxville, Iowa. A childhood friend named Bobby, who I had not seen for years, needed me to minister to him. I was not prepared for what I saw. His nurse came out wheeling him not in a wheelchair but pushing his hospital bed! She wheeled him to a visiting room and got him situated. Bobby was unable to speak, his eyes were closed, his moustache and beard were partial patches of hair, and his hands and feet curled inward as if he had suffered a stroke.

I leaned down beside him and began to visit with him. I said to him, "Bobby, it's me, John Fry. It has been a long time. I am here to talk to you about Jesus." He did not respond. I went on talking to him about our childhood days and school. He still didn't respond. So I came against any assignment the devil had against Bobby's life, and in the name of Jesus commanded the foul demon spirit afflicting him to leave. It left and I believe it brought Bobby's salvation.

I quoted Romans 10:13: "For whosoever shall call upon the name of the Lord shall be saved." I repeated it several times to Bobby. I asked Bobby to say the name "Jesus," but he did not respond. I kept encouraging him to say the name of Jesus. As I was whispering into his ear, his body stiffened and he yelled. His eyes remained closed and then he screamed out the name of Jesus. I prayed over Bobby and told him I'd see him in Heaven and then we parted. He died three days later. I believe Bobby had his "one on one" with Jesus when he cried out His name!

Wake Up Call From God

One morning shortly before 7:00 A.M. the Lord sat me up on the edge of my bed. I felt a burden to get to the jail where I am a volunteer but did not know why. It was a holiday and visits were not allowed so I called the head chaplain to ask permission. He said to go ahead. My flesh wanted to crawl back underneath those blankets to go back to sleep, but I answered the Lord's calling. I took a shower to wake up and headed to the jail. It was a holiday and it felt peculiarly quiet. I had been ministering for a couple of hours from pod to pod when I noticed in the distance a correction officer approaching me and he was leading a prisoner in shackles.

The closer he got to me I noticed the prisoner was someone I had been ministering to for years. We stopped in the hallway and I noticed the prisoner was very upset. He was crying uncontrollably. He had just received a telephone call that his twin brother had been found dead. We were allowed to go into a room alone, where he received prayer. This was no coincidence, as God had set this meeting up. God ordained that moment in time for my friend to be ministered to. Normally no one from the outside was to be in the jail that day. God truly knows our every need. We need to trust in God and know that He truly is there for us.

I Thought I Was Alone

One night while I was on an exercise track in prayer, a man approached in the distance. He was running toward me and when he passed me we noticed each other. It was apparent to both of us that we were acquaintances. I had shared a conversation with him regarding my volunteer ministry at the jail. We had discussed my ministry on the streets and discussed Jesus also. He finished his laps and then came up beside me to ask how I was doing. He asked what I was doing there on the track and I told him I was praying.

I was compelled to ask him if he was saved and he told me that he was Muslim. I then asked if he would like to know about salvation, and to my astonishment he said yes. I explained about his being born into this earth by his mother in a sinful state because of the fall of Adam and Eve in the Garden of Eden. I then went on to explain the difference in being born again in Christ Jesus.

I assured him that if he left this earth without being saved, hell would surely be his home. Salvation would mean that everything from his past would be thrown into the deepest part of the sea, where God said it would be remembered no more. I told him that he would have a clean slate and a fresh start. I explained to him that because of the blood and the broken body of Jesus, his name would be written in the Lamb's Book of Life. That night he became my brother in Christ on an outdoor running track. I listened with awe as he confessed his salvation. He

had gone from being a Muslim to becoming a resi-
dent of the Kingdom of God!

Samantha

Recently I was called to an apartment where a man had lost his wife very suddenly. They had gotten up at around 7:00 A.M. and he helped with some of her clothing. She had gone to the couch to call her mother on the telephone. The husband noticed the phone making a strange sound and went to check on it. She had passed away and the phone was on the floor, dropped from her outstretched hand. Her body was still on the couch when I arrived, as they were waiting for the medical examiner to arrive.

I prayed with the husband, knowing full well the pain he was experiencing, having gone through the same emotions myself and ministered to others that had lost loved ones. He told me she had numerous health issues and was on a lot of medication and he was certain that is what had killed her. We entered the apartment and the two of us prayed, laying our hands on her as we did. Samantha was only 29 years old and it turns out that the cause of death was a clot in her lung. She was a member of a Christian church in a nearby suburb. What an honor to be called upon even in the saddest of times, to give comfort to the grieving. A few weeks later while ministering to her husband again, I had the opportunity to lead him to the Lord.

Dad's Vision

I will never forget something that happened to my dad one beautiful summer day on our front porch. I must have been 14 or 15 years old. My brother was working beneath a car in our driveway. I was standing on our porch watching him work. I heard the door open behind me as Dad came onto the porch from the house. When the door closed I looked into my dad's eyes. I had never seen the look that was on his face that day.

He looked like he was looking off in the distance, and he turned in a circle. His face was full of amazement and he had a glow about him. He silently stood there for a while. He then shook his head as if to clear it and said to me, "Son, for as far as I could see, all I could see was the most beautiful green grass, trees, and flowers blooming. There were no buildings or houses in sight, nor concrete underneath my feet." He went to say, "Praise God, there must be a reason for Him to reveal this to me." This memory comforts me since Dad went home to be with Jesus in 1990. Please don't limit God; my Dad didn't. Dad was given a glimpse of his eternal home and I can't wait to join him there.

Salvation Across Cultures

I had a miraculous encounter with the wonder of God through a chance meeting with a family recently settled in the United States. The refugees were from Ghana, West Africa, where they were in danger for their very existence. I invited them to services at my church and afterward gave them a tour of the church facility. The tour ended in the prayer room, where I explained salvation to them.

I explained man's need for salvation due to being born into the sinful nature of mankind at of the fall of Adam and Eve in the Garden of Eden. I then asked if they would like their names written in the Lamb's Book of Life. I invited them to become my family in Christ and led them to the Lord with the Sinner's Prayer. Isn't it a miracle how God brought them to the United States to save them from physical death, only to then save them from spiritual death, in that prayer room a world away? With God there are no coincidences. This was truly ordained by God Almighty.

Letter to God

Dear God. This is one of the hardest letters I've ever had to write. I am awed by You and am at a loss for words. It is much easier to talk to you in prayer. Father, first of all I want to thank you for the precious gift of life. Life is great, even if the trials are not so enjoyable at times. Because of the blood of Your precious Son Jesus we can make it through anything. Father, before I was even in my mother's womb, You knew me. Isn't this cool, I am writing You about Your Word. I have to have more of You. You're the only one that truly fills me. I am still stuck on You.

You know what I am writing before I even think it. It gives me peace knowing that I am not alone. Father, what would You have me learn this day? How can I be used to bring You glory? What would please Your heart and give You explosive joy? Use me for Your happiness. I love the way You hold me in Your loving hands. I love how You loved me before I was living in my mother's womb. I will love You throughout my life, until I see You again. With all of my heart and soul I will love you forever. Yours truly, John.

To contact author fryclone@netzero.net

CPSIA information can be obtained at www.ICGtesting.com
Printed in the USA
LVOW090213070312

271899LV00001B/5/P